DARE
TO
WIN

JEFF CHEGWIN &
CARMELA DICLEMENTE

ILLUSTRATIONS BY KATE HAZELL

DARE
TO
WIN

LESSONS FROM 57 OF THE WORLD'S
MOST SUCCESSFUL PEOPLE

hardie grant books

CONTENTS

'ONLY THOSE WHO CAN EVER ACHIEVE

DARE TO FAIL GREATLY

GREATLY.'

ROBERT F. KENNEDY

INTRODUCTION

What does it take to dare to win?

We all harbour dreams, especially when we're young and uninhibited by ideas of failure or ridicule. And what we learn in childhood – the opportunities we're given to explore and experiment, how we manage our achievements and failures, learn resilience and stay optimistic – all contribute to later success.

However, in today's success-driven society we often tell ourselves that 'failing isn't an option'. But when we strive to excel in everything we put our minds to, if we do fail we're often so traumatised by any mistakes we make that we are blind to the lessons we could learn.

In this way, when something fails it can actually show us what we need to do next in order to succeed. What if having our egos bruised was in fact the very way in which we could come back stronger, with better solutions and a higher chance of hitting our goals? A mistake is nothing more than something we did that didn't work out in the way we wanted. We don't have to repeat our mistakes, but we should always take the opportunity to learn from them.

'It is impossible to live without failing at something, unless you live so cautiously that you might as well not have lived at all – in which case you fail by default.'

J. K. ROWLING

Most entrepreneurial go-getters who have the vision and spirit to take risks take some hard knocks along the way – it's an inevitable part of the process – but they are the eventual winners. In *Dare to Win* we hear stories from 57 of the world's most successful people.

None of them were born successful but, just like the rest of us, they've had failures, been rejected, had crises of confidence – and they all dared to get back up and try again.

Taking risks also means being true to who you are – being an individual often takes guts and courage, especially if you're not like anyone else – and, likewise, age, gender and finances should never quash your goals. As the life stories in this book demonstrate, it's important to stay positive and not become negative or bitter. So whether you've just lost your job, didn't get that promotion you wanted, have been dumped by your partner, are struggling to hit that goal, or just need a bit of inspiration, this is the book for you.

1 BE AMBITIOUS

How do you realise your dreams? How do you turn an ambition into a reality? Take a leaf out of Elvis Presley's book, a man who certainly knew all about ambition and the momentum and sheer force required to power your way to the top. He said, *'Ambition is a dream with a V8 engine.'* Of course, even a V8 engine can shudder, stall, grind to a halt. It happens to the best – even to the King of Rock 'n' Roll!

Elvis was a young, energetic performer, already displaying signs of his onstage performances that later thrilled and alarmed audiences. Elvis, though, was still developing his career, so when he was offered a slot to play at one of America's most revered music institutions, the Grand Ole Opry, he jumped at the chance. The Grand Ole Opry has been called the 'home of American music' and 'country's most famous stage', and is a Nashville institution dating back to the mid-1920s. So this performance was a very big deal.

Ol' Swivel Hips pitched up to perform at the Nashville show, on a bill headlined by Faron Young,

'Ambition is a dream with a V8 engine.'
ELVIS PRESLEY

along with class country acts the Wilburn Brothers, and Bill and Scotty. Elvis left the Opry and its audience literally 'all shook up'. They were used to a more sedate, more familiar country sound, not the antics of the gyrating Elvis.

He did not go down well with the crowd. After the show, Elvis was advised not to give up his day job – which, by the way, was as a truck driver – and told to abandon his hopes of making it in the music business. Fortunately, Elvis, with his dream powered by a metaphorical V8 engine, just put his pedal to the metal and went on to become the biggest-selling music artist of all time.

Imagine how different the world of music would be if he had given up on his dream. Imagine what the world would be like if we all just surrendered – perhaps an unexciting and muted place where no one has the power to punch through.

So, like Elvis, don't let anyone stall you on your path to fulfilment. Keep your hands on the steering wheel, keep faith in your vision and continue to motor along the highway to success.

Many in this world strive for success, and expect a few knocks and false dawns on the way to achieving it. But imagine this situation: you have already become a success, and by the age of 26 you are riding high in your chosen profession, when you are knocked sideways by a sucker punch.

That's what happened to Walt Disney. At just 26, he was already a successful animator and artist, working with the mighty Universal Studios. Their first-ever Disney creation was a character called Oswald the Lucky Rabbit. Mischievous and fun-loving, with long, floppy ears, the roguish rabbit was adored by the movie-going public, who had never before seen anything like this bouncy animated cartoon character having a riot.

Travelling to New York to catch up with the 'suits' and discuss the future, it was in Disney's mind to ask for a pay increase given Oswald's popularity. He was met with a career hand grenade. The distributor informed Disney there would be no increase; indeed, a more modest role was intended for Walt. Furthermore, Oswald the Lucky Rabbit was actually the property of the distributor and his backer – Universal Pictures.

2
FIND THE CHALLENGE IN ADVERSITY

'If you can dream it, you can do it.' *WALT DISNEY*

And here's the killer blow: they had poached most of Disney's colleagues.

Walt had a choice: give up his own studio and work for Universal, or leave without his most popular character, without the support of a mighty movie conglomerate and try to make it on his own.

It was a desperate moment, but Walt didn't give up. He went on to much bigger and better projects, starting with that inspired creation Mickey Mouse. Donald Duck, Pluto the dog and Goofy soon followed, as well as films that will always enchant – think *Mary Poppins*, *One Hundred and One Dalmatians* and *The Jungle Book*.

'All the adversity I've had in my life, all my troubles and obstacles, have strengthened me ... You may not realise it when it happens, but a kick in the teeth may be the best thing in the world for you.'

To paraphrase Walt Disney, when faced with adversity, don't lose heart. Failure has a way of freezing us and making us feel fearful and lost. It may seem perverse, but try to see a setback as a boon. Seize it and learn from it – it will strengthen you for the future.

3 FOCUS

'I'm encouraging other people, whether they're professionals or not, to use their creativity to express themselves, to get a conversation going, to get the party started, really.'
MADONNA

Life's journey is not an easy one. Every single person on this planet will face challenges daily; sometimes they can be huge, such as losing a partner, child or your home, not having enough to eat, worrying about paying the bills, or just feeling desperate – the black dog of depression. Whatever the size or scale of the crisis, if it's happening to you, it is the biggest of troubles right then.

How do we react? Withdraw from our surroundings, brood over the dilemma, become atrophied with anxiety? Probably. But there is another option, what we might call the 'Madonna method'.

Madonna's career as a performance artist (never call her a pop star unless you want to annoy her) has spanned four decades. Has she always been lauded, feted and admired? Definitely not. Has that stopped her? Not at all.

Her debut decade, the 1980s, saw her become a hit with audiences worldwide when she popped up at Live Aid and performed 'Holiday', introduced by Bette Midler in typically witty and waspish style: *'We are thrilled to be able to introduce you to… a woman who occasionally pulled herself up by her bra straps and has been known to let them down occasionally.'*

Torrid times have followed. Many of her songs – especially 'Like a Virgin', 'Like a Prayer', 'Justify My Love' and 'Papa Don't Preach' – have provoked outrage and controversy. She's bared flesh on more than one occasion, is liberal with the f-word, brought S&M fashion into the mainstream way before *Fifty Shades of Grey*, and has created iconic moments through style statements – who can forget the conical Gaultier bra she wore on her 1990 Blond Ambition World Tour?

Is the Madonna of today slowing down, seeking a more modest role in music, toning down her performances? Not really. Her Rebel Heart Tour was her tenth worldwide concert tour. It concluded in Australia in March 2016, garnering reviews such as the *Washington Post*'s 'as provocative as ever' and earning five stars from the *Guardian*. The backdrop to this was a painful custody battle over her and Guy Ritchie's son, Rocco. She also had to deal with the barbed comments about her adoption of two children from Malawi.

Madonna doesn't falter, she gets the party started, she sings her socks off, wows audiences, wins praise for her artistry and continues to reinvent both her look and sound. She has combined home life, marriage and children with the demands of her profession. Think of the energy and painstaking concentration and planning required to fill stadia, make hit after hit record, stay relevant and remain a huge star for decades.

Think the Madonna way – do your absolute best and 'get the party started'!

4

'ANYONE WHO MADE A MISTAKE TRIED

HAS NEVER

HAS NEVER

ANYTHING NEW.'

EINSTEIN

The quote below by Steve Jobs encapsulates the key message that you have to trust, have faith, even if there seems little that is solid around you. Trusting, believing in something that is a comfort, reassures you that all will work out well in the end.

Steve Jobs' birth parents were educated, of comfortable middle-class stock. His birth mother grew up on a farm in Wisconsin and his father was an immigrant from Syria. Their romance resulted in a pregnancy, rather shocking for 1950s America, and even more scandalous because they were an interracial couple.

They had hoped to place their baby with a graduate couple, in the hope of guaranteeing an academic future for their offspring. That adoption fell through, and their baby boy found a home with a blue-collar couple, Paul and Clara Jobs.

Steve Jobs was not in the least hampered by his start in life, so far away from that of his college-educated birth parents. Paul Jobs was a machinist working for a company in what much later became the centre of the tech sector – Silicon Valley – and his young adoptive son Steve would watch his father's handiwork with fascination.

Fast-forward to the 1990s and beyond, when Steve Jobs gained fame as the legendary force behind one of the most recognised brands in the world – Apple. Even though he grew up without his biological father, he went on to be regarded as 'the father of the digital revolution'.

An irregular start in life, not knowing one of your birth parents, is enough to disrupt, destabilise, even destroy the hope of a happy future. But sometimes just trusting in yourself, as Steve Jobs did, is all you need to truly achieve.

5
TRUST YOURSELF

'You have to trust in something – your gut, destiny, life, karma, whatever. This approach has never let me down, and it has made all the difference in my life.'

STEVE JOBS

6
RECLAIM CRITICISM

'The most alluring thing a woman can have is confidence.'
BEYONCÉ

When you look at yourself in the mirror in the morning what do you see? Do you see a refreshed, luminous face ready to start the new day, or is your reaction quite negative? Do you see a tired, stale face full of imperfections?

It is well known that women are more critical of themselves than men – though men are catching up in the self-disparaging stakes, fretting about their looks and muscles in the way that women do about their weight and sexiness, according to a comprehensive study by Chapman University in California. But it is women in particular who are prone to self-censure. They are encouraged to pick at their perceived blemishes through the pressure of public evaluation and the media.

The rich and famous do not elude this scrutiny. Beyoncé is one of the world's most successful female solo artists, famed for her powerful voice as well as her curvaceous figure.

She's been slammed for her curves and other body parts too. One well-known British actor even said that Beyoncé has 'elephant ankles'.

Her response to the fat flak can be heard in the 2001 song 'Bootylicious', hitting back at the pressure to be super-thin: *'It's a celebration of curves and a celebration of women's bodies.'* It reached number two in the UK singles chart.

What both men and women can glean from Beyoncé's example is that it's better to respond to an insult creatively rather than whinge or whine. Take the flak and use it, reclaim the criticism and create a banner that you and others can rally around. Channel the frustrations and feelings of injustice into a productive reply that explains without being defensive; convert through charisma and win the argument with wit.

'When I'm not feeling my best I ask myself, "What are you gonna do about it?" I use the negativity to fuel the transformation into a better me.'

7
STEP OUTSIDE YOUR COMFORT ZONE

'I think I survive because I don't limit myself. If there's some experience I want to have or place I want to go, I do it.'
LEONARDO DICAPRIO

How hard are you willing to push yourself in the pursuit of an ideal? We are cosy in our comfort zone, but are we capable of stepping beyond it, hovering on the pain barrier and even venturing beyond?

We become conditioned to staying within safe parameters, limiting stress and discomfort. But do we need to push ourselves mentally and physically beyond that zone in order to achieve success? Early work in this area by American psychologists Robert Yerkes and John Dodson observed that performance

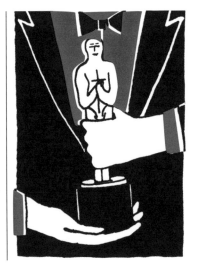

increases with mental and physical stimulation; however, if we are overstimulated, performance dips. Thus we have the Yerkes–Dodson law of 1908.

Actor Leonardo DiCaprio was brought up in the rough part of Hollywood. Drug dealing and prostitution were among the unsavoury activities to which the young DiCaprio was exposed – perhaps not the most conventional grounding for Hollywood stardom.

Previously nominated four times for an acting award (and once for producing), he finally won his first Oscar in 2016 for *The Revenant*. In the film he plays fur trapper Hugh Glass, who is savagely attacked by a bear, eats the raw liver from a bison and ends up sleeping in an animal carcass, illustrating the tough, often gruesome existence of the early frontiersmen.

DiCaprio, who performed many of his own stunts, has described the film as 'physically gruelling'. Shot in natural light on location, the scenes in which we see DiCaprio plunging into freezing rivers actually happened. He'd then be thawed out by the equivalent of a giant hairdryer to stop his joints seizing up with the cold. The film is a jaw-dropping, awe-inspiring experience.

Despite starring in many great movies, such as *What's Eating Gilbert Grape*, *Titanic*, *The Wolf of Wall Street*, *Django Unchained* and *The Beach*, it was the harrowing ultra-realism of *The Revenant* that brought him his first Academy Award, for Best Actor.

DiCaprio leapt out of his comfort zone, literally, and it paid huge dividends and won him acclaim.

In the words of Dr Brené Brown, a research professor in the Graduate College of Social Work at the University of Houston who has spent many years studying vulnerability, courage, worthiness and shame: *'We can choose courage or we can choose comfort, but we can't have both.'*

It takes massive courage to push yourself into the most difficult and uncomfortable situations, but beyond there may be rewards – you'll only know by venturing there, so don't wait!

Owning yourself, knowing yourself, accepting yourself. How far are you willing to push your quest for self-awareness? How honest are you really? Honest enough to defy convention, jeopardise a great reputation and lay yourself open to the most brutal public scrutiny?

Caitlyn Jenner, formerly known as Bruce, was a massive star in the 1970s, a tremendous athlete who broke the world record for the decathlon at the 1976 Montreal Olympics. The story of her journey from Olympic icon to transgender woman is one that has gripped the public imagination.

It became front-page news around the world when Bruce Jenner's new identity was unveiled on the front cover of *Vanity Fair* magazine's July 2015 issue. Caitlyn Jenner was revealed, a beautiful and luminous individual. The transitioning process is not for the faint-hearted, but living as Bruce for 65 years was even more uncomfortable – a half

existence; the constant struggle with feelings of shame and confusion; the battle to keep the truth buried deep.

When awarded the Arthur Ashe Courage Award in 2015, Jenner commented: *'I trained hard, I competed hard, and for that people respected me. But this transition has been harder on me than anything I could imagine, and that's the case for so many others besides me. For that reason alone, trans people deserve something vital – they deserve your respect.'*

Courage is not only about playing the hero, showing off, or being physically strong. It is also about being brave even when terrified. More importantly, courage should reflect wisdom and love. The transition that Bruce underwent to become Caitlyn is not something many of us will experience, but transitioning in a broader sense is definitely a process we all need to go through, to identify who we really are and how we want to live our lives. The alternative, almost too unbearable to contemplate, could be a life of regret.

8 OWN WHO YOU ARE

'If I was lying on my deathbed and I had kept this secret and never, ever did anything about it, I would be lying there saying, "You just blew your entire life. You never dealt with yourself".'

CAITLYN JENNER

Getting fired from your job can be devastating. Your self-esteem plummets and your bank account too. It is a truly traumatic experience that leaves you feeling shocked, upset and confused.

Author of the phenomenally successful *Harry Potter* books, J. K. Rowling is one of many now famous and extremely rich individuals who have in the past been given the sack. In the case of J. K. Rowling, she was working as a secretary in the London office of Amnesty International.

While the team toiled away fighting injustice, she would surreptitiously type away at her computer, developing her fabulous stories and characters. It wasn't long before her bosses rumbled her, and J. K. was politely shown the door. But she's in good company: luminaries dismissed from their jobs include *Vogue*'s editor-in-chief Anna Wintour, Sean Combs (aka Puff

9
WHEN YOU HIT ROCK BOTTOM, LOOK UP

'It is impossible to live without failing at something, unless you live so cautiously that you might as well not have lived at all – in which case you fail by default.'

J. K. ROWLING

Daddy, P. Diddy etc), Jerry Seinfeld and Oprah Winfrey.

Add to this a failed marriage, along with shocking finances that brought poverty to her door, and you can see that J. K. has had to overcome many setbacks. So her huge fortune and constant appearance on the *Sunday Times* Rich List is most gratifying – the dud office worker became a literary doyenne!

What we can take away from J. K.'s story is that failure in one sphere might release us into what we are truly destined to become. Global literary success, or indeed any achievement on this scale, might elude most of us. However, it is not the size of the accomplishment that matters, but the fact that you have fulfilled the ambition.

'Had I really succeeded at anything else, I might never have found the determination to succeed in the one arena I believed I truly belonged.'

10

'MISTAKES ARE THE PORTALS OF

DISCO

JAMES JOYCE

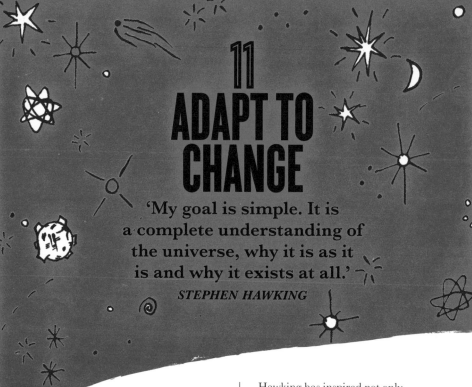

11
ADAPT TO CHANGE

'My goal is simple. It is
a complete understanding of
the universe, why it is as it
is and why it exists at all.'

STEPHEN HAWKING

Much has been written about the extraordinary life and work of physicist and polymath Stephen Hawking. Who else could ever think of tackling a topic as enormous, infinite and esoteric as the one he explored in his book *A Brief History of Time*, first published in 1988? He has followed up this ground-breaking work with *A Briefer History of Time* and *The Universe in a Nutshell*.

Hawking has inspired not only scientists but also ordinary people around the world, who admire him for his great intellect and his refusal to be hampered by a degenerative condition called amyotrophic lateral sclerosis (ALS), commonly known as motor neurone disease in the UK. Incidentally, ALS is also referred to as Lou Gehrig disease, after the Yankees baseball legend who died from the then unnamed condition at the age of 37.

Hawking, gradually paralysed by the condition and now confined to a

wheelchair, is able to communicate his profound and often jokey thoughts through muscle movement in his cheek which is translated by a speech-generating device.

Hawking was 21 when he was diagnosed with ALS and he was not expected to live more than a few years. He has defied this prognosis, and his condition, and continued to contribute enormously to our understanding of the universe – of our very existence.

While we may not be gifted with an intellect that drives us to try to answer what are probably the biggest questions of all – 'Why are we here?' and 'How did we get here?' – that does not mean we cannot still aim high, perhaps even for the stars in our own universe, as Stephen Hawking does. Let's be inspired by him and this thought: *'Intelligence is the ability to adapt to change.'*

After all, his passion for knowledge has eclipsed any frailty.

12
BUILD ON SUCCESS

'Success is a lousy teacher. It seduces smart people into thinking they can't lose.'
BILL GATES

How much success is enough? Does ambition have a ceiling? When do you know that you've made it? Our tendency is to rest up when we've made a huge effort and tasted success. This happens even on a domestic level: you cook a fabulous meal, so it's time for someone else to roll up their sleeves and do the washing-up, right?

Maybe not.

Certainly not if you're Bill Gates, one of the cleverest and richest men in the world, and synonymous with the giant software company Microsoft.

His aptitude for technology began to show when he was still at school. As a teenager, he developed a simple online game that allowed pupils to play against the school computer. It was a version of what we call noughts and crosses or tic-tac-toe.

Not long after, he teamed up with school friend Paul Allen and they developed a computer programme. Traf-O-Data monitored traffic patterns in their home city of Seattle. It was a bit of a flop, so for Bill Gates it was time to move on to the next thing – a software programme for the computer MITS Altair. Micro-soft, as it was then known, was born.

mind-boggling riches, Bill Gates has never rested on his laurels; not for him getting caught out by the changing tastes of consumers or being a step behind developments in what is probably the fastest-moving sector.

Gates shows us that we should never, ever think, 'This is it'; that we should be wary of the soporific effect that achievement can bring. Staying hungry for success relies on constantly pushing yourself and those around you to work harder.

Very soon sales hit the $1 million mark, then exceeded it. Having dropped out of Harvard, one of the prestigious Ivy League universities, to pursue his entrepreneurial goals, Bill Gates pushed on and in a few more years, when just 31, he became a billionaire. Eight years later he was the richest man in the world.

Bill Gates is said to be incredibly driven and meticulous in his work, regularly working unfeasibly long hours to realise his dreams. He could be tricky and heated – signs, perhaps, of his passion for his work, his belief that what he was doing was indeed a world game changer.

It certainly was. Despite the

13
TAKE CARE OF YOUR MENTAL HEALTH

'Self-pity is the worst possible emotion anyone can have. And the most destructive.'
STEPHEN FRY

W e all feel a bit low at some points in our life. Who doesn't feel like burrowing into the duvet when the sun disappears or the season changes to cold and grey? This is a mild form of what can be a seriously debilitating condition that could stymie your success. It can even hijack your happiness when seemingly you have it all. What then?

Whether it is a mild depression or a more profound mental health issue, many of us are or will be affected at some stage in our lives. Actress Catherine Zeta-Jones has revealed she is bipolar, actor Robin Williams' battle with his inner demons led to him taking his own life, comedienne Ruby Wax continues to work with her condition, and actor and writer Stephen Fry has attempted suicide.

Fry, who famously went AWOL from the West End play in which he was starring in 1995, is now a highly visible ambassador for depressive conditions and invests a lot of energy in battling the stigma around mental health. He's president of the mental health charity MIND and has done a great deal to shine a spotlight on a bleak side of life, one that has been largely hidden through people's shame and fear of being labelled a 'loony'.

As he says: *'This is not a condition that is ever going to go away... No matter how well things seem to be going, there's always the possibility of me getting it wrong.'*

Our mental health can be fragile; it could disrupt or destroy our careers and home life. We are all susceptible to being derailed by depression; it is not fussy about who it targets, or when it might strike. The good news is that we are not alone – it is survivable and not a curse, just a condition of being alive on this earth with its myriad challenges and rewards.

14 STAY CURIOUS

'It's a discipline. Make yourself be happy, and then, funnily enough, you'll be happy.'
JOANNA LUMLEY

She played one of the most reprobate characters on TV, demanding Bolly and cigarettes and proud of not having eaten since 1974 – destroying everything in her path, appreciating little and always wanting more. Joanna Lumley's character Patsy Stone appeared in the TV sitcom *Ab Fab*, with a film version out too.

But the bored, rude, drunken, bitchy and superficial Patsy could not be further from the real-life Joanna.

Joanna Lumley is involved with

a huge number of charities; has championed the cause of Nepalese fighting force, the Gurkhas; has experienced being a single mum strapped for cash; has fallen out with and made up with her sister; and declared *'There's something rather thrilling about being 70'*.

She is regarded as a national treasure. No slouch, she happily uses her platform to champion the opinions and the causes she holds dear, as well as to urge young women not to drink so much that they end up being *'sick in the gutter'*. But she's also a legacy star who was named as one of the most powerful women in the UK by Radio 4's *Women's Hour*.

Joanna Lumley embodies so many of the qualities we should all admire – from her sense of justice in fighting the corner of an unfashionable cause, to her embracing of ageing as a reward for life and her simple home truths about happiness.

15 BE THE GOAT, NOT THE SHEEP

'Part of me suspects I'm a loser, and the other part of me thinks I'm God Almighty.'

JOHN LENNON

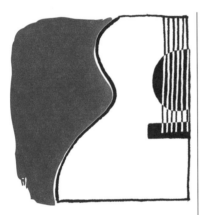

Are you a wild child? Do your mind and spirit work in a different way from most of the people around you, and do you find yourself always getting the blame?

It is a difficult thing to be out on a limb and to keep your natural sense of fun and originality flowing. After all, there is only so much criticism and telling-off you can take before your core starts to collapse.

But hold firm. A young lad by the name of John Lennon came in for a lot of flak when attending Quarry Bank school in Liverpool. His teachers tried to suppress the live wire that was John Lennon, who was showing no sign then that he would become part of one of the greatest bands the world has ever seen – The Beatles.

At school he was constantly told off, chastised, rounded on and berated for his lack of attention and inability to sit still. He was a challenging pupil whose claim to fame was that he received three detention slips in one day – not once, but twice!

He was described as being 'rather a clown in class' and accused of 'wasting other pupils' time'. The list of misdemeanours included 'sabotage', 'fighting in class', 'nuisance', 'shoving' and 'just no interest whatsoever'.

The clown became a global star alongside his Beatles bandmates. They were the first British group to break into America and to have a teenage fan hysteria named after them – Beatlemania. Ever jocular and mischievous, even into adulthood, this quip at the group's 1963 Royal Variety Performance in front of the Queen Mother and Princess Margaret illustrates how

witty Lennon could be: *'Will the people in the cheaper seats clap your hands? And the rest of you, if you'll just rattle your jewellery.'*

Looking back, you might think these are exactly the traits that helped propel John Lennon to stardom. 'Naughty' can be a catch-all word we use to describe behaviour that is challenging. But it might also point to a deep self-belief and sense of conviction in the kind of world a person wishes to inhabit. Naughty might be a way of saying someone is original or energetic and unafraid to go against the grain. It shows ambition and is a way of developing some of those attributes we laud so much in our idols – originality, purpose, surprise, eccentricity and unconventionality. So, remember this: a bad school report or appraisal might actually contain the clues to your strengths.

How many of us have managed to turn a job rejection into an offer? It's likely that many of us have never even thought about continuing to press for a post that we have already been passed on.

We should look to the creator of the Starbucks coffee chain for inspiration. His beginnings were humble, growing up as he did in the projects of Brooklyn – the low-cost housing schemes that became synonymous with social deprivation, crime and violence. His parents worked hard but never seemed to have much money, a lesson Howard Schultz observed.

After attending college, Schultz worked for a kitchenware company and was intrigued when a small retailer in Seattle put in a large order for slow-drip coffee machines. He visited the small Starbucks store in Seattle, which was crammed full of sacks of coffee beans from exotic places – was it the coffee aromas from all over the world that turned his head? Whatever the reason, Schultz was excited by what he saw. He envisioned a network of quality coffee outlets and set about persuading the three Starbucks owners to hire him. They said 'no way', the scale of Schultz's plan being far beyond what they were comfortable with, which was retailing the beans and selling the machines.

Schultz just wouldn't take no for an answer. Pitching the concept again, he tried to engage the Starbucks trio and point out how the business could grow. They brought him into the fold, briefly, before his ambition outgrew his environment.

So Schultz went and started his own chain of coffee houses, Il Giornale. They became a success and in a very short time he was able to buy his beloved original Starbucks shop and the name, which was the start of the mighty Starbucks Coffee Company, one of the largest chains in the world.

Schultz remained solid and convinced that his vision was realisable, despite the rejections and 'this can't be done' attitudes he encountered. He used his belief and every scrap of perseverance to push on through to make his dream of a café culture real. Like him, don't take no to mean the end. It may be that a particular avenue has closed, but look beyond the negative and seek out other means to reach your goal. Stay focused and try not to lose heart.

16
HAVE A VISION

'Most people, when turned down for a job,
just go away... I've had to use every ounce
of perseverance to make it happen.'

HOWARD SCHULTZ

17

'YOU'LL NEVER FIND A RAINBO

W IF YOU'RE LOOKING DOWN.'

CHARLIE
CHAPLIN

Success attracts excess. It encourages your ego. *The X Factor* and *Britain's Got Talent* reality TV shows are the creation of Simon Cowell, the music and entertainment mogul who has influenced our viewing tastes for decades. From One Direction to Little Mix, Susan Boyle to Leona Lewis and Jedward, these household names were created by his shows, which have the power to transform the lives of contestants, ordinary people who are launched into galactic stardom.

Simon Cowell seems confident, cocksure even. He is charismatic with a certain bravura, which you surely need to rise through the ranks and become a supremo in your chosen field.

Immense power can also lead to feelings of invulnerability. He's the exec who let a young Kylie Minogue, fresh out of Australia, wait in reception... He passed on Take That and was pointed in his criticism of the lead singer, who

18
LEARN THE LESSON AND START AGAIN

'I've had many failures. The biggest were at times when I believed my own hype.'
SIMON COWELL

he judged to be too overweight: *'I said I'll sign them without the fat one.'* Ahem, that's national treasure Gary Barlow he's talking about.

Now in his fifties, Cowell is fabulously wealthy and feted wherever he goes. He's supremely self-assured, of course, but he has tasted the bitterness of failure. In 1989 he made and lost a fortune, forfeited everything and was forced to move back home to live with his mum. He admits he had been rather caught up in the whole flashiness

of having loads of money. Cowell was, as the cliché goes, a victim of his own success. But he grappled his way back to be the mega-millionaire of today.

It is easy to feel invincible when a huge amount of success comes your way, but that can lead to arrogance which can in turn make you out of step with those around you, and the inevitable stumble can become one almighty fall from grace. Salutary lessons sometimes just have to be learnt the hard way.

19 BE RESILIENT

'You need a stubborn belief in an idea in order to see it realised.'
SIR JAMES DYSON

Sir James Dyson is the genius inventor and re-inventor of eponymous products, including his best-known creation – the bagless vacuum cleaner. This one invention alone was five years in the making and there were thousands of attempts to get it right before he finally did! Of course, there are many more Dyson products that are almost as ubiquitous.

He believed in his revolutionary vacuum cleaner and, armed with the final prototype, sought to collaborate with Amway in the US. Dyson describes it as a 'disaster'. So he remortgaged his house to raise capital and set up his own manufacturing company, Dyson Ltd.

Still having problems getting store space and distributors onboard, Dyson collared a politician visiting his factory, bemoaning the lack of access to big electronics stores such as Comet. That politician's wife was on the board of Comet. Very soon, Dyson vacuums were in their shops and became the best-selling vacuum on the market.

The brand is recognised around the world, the company is hugely successful, and James Dyson is a very rich man. He took enormous risks because he believed absolutely in his creation. Being resilient when slated and striving for perfection are essential elements for conquering the critics and seizing victory.

20
SPEAK
UP

'There is prejudice. It is a problem and I can't go along any more with brushing it under the carpet. This business is about selling, and blonde and blue-eyed girls are what sells.'

NAOMI CAMPBELL

It is not easy to be a spokesperson. In many organisations you are not rewarded for being outspoken, drawing attention to corporate failings, corruption or prejudice. But isn't it right to vocalise those shortcomings, regardless of the cost?

Mention of the supermodel Naomi Campbell provokes many reactions – admiration for her beauty, disdain for the prima donna behaviour, dismay at the thought she might be a bully. She may seem an odd choice for a role model, but you will see why.

The circumstances of her upbringing are well known. She was raised single-handedly by her mum, her father having skipped away before she was even born. Home was south London, which at that time was gritty and not gentrified like it is today.

Her most important contribution to society could be this: Naomi Campbell has confronted head-on the racism in the fashion world that stops women of colour being shown off, cooed over and paid as much as their blonde, blue-eyed colleagues.

She has the guts to point to her friend Kate Moss and ask why Moss can be a cover girl for *Vogue* magazine 24 times while she has

only had the starring role eight times. She questions the fashion business for not using more women of colour on the catwalk, and laments the anecdotes from the newbies who say make-up artists can't prep their skin because they're so used to working on white models.

In 2014, only 6.8 per cent of models in runway shows around the world were of colour.

We're not all supermodels, but we will all have moments where we are witness to injustice or discrimination. We shouldn't shy away from highlighting the issue; after all, it's part of a modern society that, in order to evolve, attitudes are challenged. The bias could be an oversight, a case of people not being aware or understanding that there is a problem. Don't let your role at work or home limit your sense of justice.

Hissy fits aside, Naomi Campbell's challenges to inequity are admirable.

21 USE EMOTIONAL PAIN CREATIVELY

'My music is based on personal experience, so I have to live a little before I can write anything. It took a break-up to get me going. When I'm happy, I don't have much to write about.'

ADELE

Turning pain into art might not appeal. But no pain no gain, right? There's a myth around creative people that they have to suffer for their art – the rejections, damning criticisms of their talent, the awful reviews, the snipes, barbs and insults. But is it a myth? Perhaps pain is the cauldron from which extraordinary work can flow...

For the British singer Adele, torment has been a rich source of creativity. Her broken relationships and ruminations on the fickleness of love have propelled her to global superstar status. The London girl with the voice that can melt hearts and fill arenas found fame and fortune with the 2008 release of her first album, *19*.

We know that a single from the album was 'Chasing Pavements', a song inspired by a row with her boyfriend. After the heated confrontation with him, Adele found herself trudging through the lonely London streets wondering what to do, what life was about, when into her head came the line, 'You're chasing an empty pavement.' She laid down the track the minute she returned home and it went on to be a number one hit around the world.

Discomfort in life, her faith in love shaken and a bruised heart have resulted in more wildly popular albums, plus an Oscar for the theme song to the Bond movie *Skyfall*.

It's not necessary to deliberately court disaster or upset in order to have some creative grist for your mill, but try instead to use those moments of intense emotion (or pain) to reflect more deeply on the nature of existence. We may not all be an Adele, transforming lows into global highs, but the experience of deep reflection at a crucial moment is invaluable to each and every one of us.

22 ROLL UP YOUR SLEEVES AND GRAFT

'Talent is cheaper than table salt. What separates the talented individual from the successful one is a lot of hard work.'

STEPHEN KING

We all have talent; some have more and some less. Talents are unique – there is no one else on the planet with quite the same gift as you have. Not all talent blooms, or is recognised, or feted.

Horror writer Stephen King's first book, *The Long Walk*, flopped. Undeterred, he hunkered down and set about writing the next one.

A few books down the line and without a bestseller, Stephen King was alarmingly broke. He got by teaching English and working manual jobs in the semester breaks to earn some cash for his wife and young family.

He didn't flag, or throw in the towel. He kept on working hard and writing in between his jobs and family life, until his big break came with the horror classic *Carrie* in 1974. The rest we know – many bestsellers followed, including *The Shining*, *Misery*, *Salem's Lot* and *It*, as well as blockbuster movies such as *Creepshow* and *The Shawshank Redemption*.

To thrive in your chosen field, you really do have to roll up your sleeves and graft your way to success. Talent alone does not automatically mean you'll climb the ladder. In the words of the 19th-century French novelist Émile Zola: *'The artist is nothing without the gift, but the gift is nothing without the work.'*

23

'WE HAVE FORTY REASONS BUT NOT A SINGLE

MILLION FOR FAILURE, EXCUSE.'

RUDYARD KIPLING

24 STAND BY YOUR BELIEFS AND PRINCIPLES

'Only a man who knows what it is like to be defeated can reach down to the bottom of his soul and come up with the extra ounce of power it takes to win when the match is even.'
MUHAMMAD ALI

There is a fine line between aggression and assertiveness. We often confuse the two, and when confronted with an uncomfortable truth we may default to labelling the unnerving behaviour as aggression when it is not.

Courage is another characteristic that we can lazily define as simply being 'brave'. But courage is more complex: it is being brave, of course, but it's also being smart, knowing when to weigh in and when to pull back. And, on a wider philosophical level, courage is ultimately bound up with broader social principles such as justice, fairness and equality.

In 2016, the world lost a champion when Muhammad Ali passed away. He was a global superstar, a boxing legend, who managed to turn what some see as a brutal sport into an art form. He could be aggressive – he had to be as a world-class fighter – and at times he was merciless in the ring.

But Ali was a fighter outside the ring too, for racial equality, peace and tolerance. In 1964, Ali was known to the world as Cassius Clay – he called it his 'slave name'. After converting to Islam, he rejected the name, explaining that, *'Clay only meant dirt…'* whereas: *'I am Muhammad Ali, a free name – it means beloved of God.'*

The Nation of Islam was viewed with suspicion and fear and this was a risky move, but he did it proudly. Ali made another bold public statement when, asserting his Muslim values, he refused to be drafted into the US Army: *'Under no conditions do we take part in wars and take the lives of other humans.'* It was 1967 and the war in Vietnam was raging, with the US supporting the South in their fight against the Communist North.

The principle of peace would cost him his world heavyweight title, see his career in tatters and his liberty threatened.

Ali further used his fame for good, raising money for research into Parkinson's, the disease that claimed his life, and he was made a Messenger of Peace by the United Nations for his work with developing countries. Many other causes also benefited from Ali's support. His mere presence at an event would draw huge crowds and generate funds.

Muhammad Ali – beautiful exponent of the noble art of boxing – shows us by his own example that a true champion can control and channel his power; he can apply it appropriately, and with intelligence, tolerance and philanthropy, to be a defender of all.

25
OVERCOME REJECTION

'Most successes are unhappy. That's why they are successes – they have to reassure themselves about themselves by achieving something that the world will notice.'

AGATHA CHRISTIE

'No thank you' are three of the most hurtful words. We hear and see them a lot in different contexts but they always mean rejection. Seemingly innocuous, these words can strike at the very core of our being, politely telling us that we are worthless, our endeavour pathetic, our talent non-existent.

Did you know that the queen of crime fiction, Agatha Christie, endured years of rejection from publishers before she finally struck a book deal? She appears in the *Guinness Book of Records* as the world's best-selling author, with two billion copies of her novels sold worldwide.

We are grateful to that publisher. Christie gifted us countless gripping thrillers and two terrific detective characters in the refined Belgian Hercule Poirot and the unassuming sleuth Miss Marple of St Mary Mead, said to be based on

her grandmother. When he died in the book *Curtain: Poirot's Last Case*, Hercule Poirot was given a full-page obituary in the *New York Times*.

Her thrillers inevitably included a murder around which the mystery ensued – you might say she created the 'whodunnit'. Various means are deployed to bump off characters, and she had a professional knowledge of poisons, having qualified as a dispenser in 1917.

So the next time you receive a 'No thank you', or even hundreds of them, cast your mind back to Agatha Christie's years of rejection. To continue to court rebuffs might not appeal; but giving up is certainly the end of the dream.

When you feel like flaking out on a task, think of the words of scientist Thomas Edison: *'Our greatest weakness lies in giving up. The most certain way to succeed is always to try just one more time.'*

26
MAKE HAPPY ACCIDENTS

'I got to be known as Mr Persistent, because I wouldn't give up.'
SPENCER SILVER

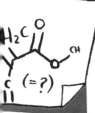

We all know the saying 'to strike gold', meaning to get lucky and make a fortune. One organic chemist called Spencer Silver turned glue into gold when he accidentally created an adhesive that was sticky, but not so sticky that it would set.

Working for the company 3M in the late 60s, he was part of a research team looking into adhesives with a simple directive – to make the strongest bonding agent they could. In fact, Silver unintentionally created something rather weak. The idea evolved to spray the substance on to a board, to which you could stick and remove pieces of paper. And there the idea stuck, as Silver spent the next few years trying to figure out how best to use the 'high-tack, low-peel' stuff. He would give lectures to colleagues in 3M hoping to pique their interest in the adhesive, never flagging in his proselytising.

One such co-worker was Art Fry, who would nail the brilliance of the

product and solve a little problem he had too. Fry was in a church choir but was always losing his place in his hymn book. He remembered Silver's eulogising about his adhesive substance, and thought how great it'd be to make a gummy paper that would stay in place and could be removed without causing damage. Hey presto – the sticky note was born, known around the globe as the Post-It note.

They are everywhere, a permanent fixture in the stationery cupboard and an essential for many of us who just like leaving a note knowing it won't blow away. Post-Its are a joy.

Happy accidents can lead to wonderful discoveries. No one even knew the world was missing small, colourful, sticky bits of reusable paper until they appeared on the market. Silver had the adhesive and persevered with his belief in it. He met Art Fry – someone who could come in with fresh ideas for a practical use for the product. That's how you make the duo who created the ubiquitous Post-It.

27 DON'T LET OTHERS DEFINE YOU

'I want to be treated
as a person, not as a
woman or a man.'

JACK MONROE

Breaking the rules and daring to be different always attracts censure from one quarter or another. Historically, this criticism would have been conveyed in print, in a newspaper or magazine. Or indeed, via a TV programme, happy to whip up the crowd and stoke indignation. Of course, other outlets are now open to our would-be critics. We have social media through which to express outrage or disgust, with Twitter to deliver immediate, pithy, though not always eloquent, sentiments.

Jack Monroe is known as a food blogger, a cookbook author specialising in budget recipes, a mother. Jack has lived on the breadline. Jack has defied conventions and attracted a heap of nastiness via various platforms, some of it aimed specifically at the very essence of what defines a person – their gender identity. Jack's own definition, of being a non-binary transgender individual, rattled many people's cages and destabilised Jack's most intimate relationships.

'I'm a little bit female and a little bit male. Finally, I fit in my skin.'

Jack is now cautiously optimistic, especially when it comes to expressing gender identity; and in 2015, on receiving the Women of the Future Award in the media category, quipped, *'I'm not sure I'll even* be *a woman in the future!'*

Sometimes when we're trying to define ourselves it can look from the outside as just wilfully defying convention. But don't allow lazy labels like 'rebel', or even 'freak', to distract you from your intention to be an individual, to be your individual.

28

'YOUR TIME IS LIMITED,

DON'T

WASTE IT

IT
LIVING SOMEONE
ELSE'S LIFE.'

STEVE JOBS

Are you an angel or a demon? Do you feel you are a good person but you are condemned by those around you for being less than pure, not quite perfect, a fake goody two-shoes? Or indeed are there times when you fall from grace, show your very human failings? We grapple with many conflicting sides of our persona, and can struggle to stay centred while, within, all is in turmoil.

We owe some of our theories on human nature and original sin to a 4th-century thinker – Augustine. The 18th century saw philosopher Jean-Jacques Rousseau propose that mankind is essentially good. For a very modern illustration of this struggle within ourselves, we need look no further than Ariana Grande. The American child star, who progressed from shows on kids' TV channel Nickelodeon to being a contemporary singer, commonly earns the title of 'pop diva'.

From reports of her life coach quitting because of her unruliness, to her demands to be carried when tired of walking and the famous doughnut-licking 'I hate America' video, her reputation has taken a battering since her early innocent days on children's TV.

Can she really be such a brat? Or is it simply that she tries to do her best, and occasionally lapses, as we all do?

The jury is still out, but let's look to Ariana herself for a steer on her soul:

'If you want to call me a diva I'll say, "Um, well, cool." Barbra Streisand is a diva; that's amazing. Celine Dion is a diva; thank you. But if you want to call me a bitch, that's not accurate. Because it's just not in my nature.'

Our nature in its happy neutrality is not nasty, not mean or demonic. Neither is it completely altruistic, pure and good. But that's OK; that's what a human being is.

29 IGNORE THE HATERS

'But in the end, all we're responsible for is ourselves. We have to remember who we are and never question ourselves if someone else disapproves.'

ARIANA GRANDE

30 PUSH THE BOUNDARIES

We hear a lot about 'breaking the mould', shedding the familiar and even destroying it so that something new and beautiful might arise. This image is, of course, based on the classical myth of the phoenix. When nearing the end of its life cycle, it would build a nest that would burst into flames, with the bird emerging renewed and invigorated from the fire.

But if we look at the career of the biggest star of the silent movie era, Charlie Chaplin, we can see in him a maverick talent whose love of experimentation saw him push the boundaries, not so much breaking the rules of cinema at that time, but evolving them.

He appeared on screen as a tragicomic hero, basking in the bathos of the noble losers he portrayed. His characters were not caesars at the head of legions, nor were they princes pursuing a holy cause. He made the mundane, almost drab lives of ordinary people box-office gold, imbuing their stories with drama, significance and poignancy. From being hauled over giant cogs in *Modern Times* to eating his own boots in *The Gold Rush*, his genius was comedy, and it was fresh.

'Life is a tragedy when seen in close-up, but a comedy in long-shot.'
CHARLIE CHAPLIN

Cinema in the early 20th century, though silent (sound technology was limited until 1927, when *The Jazz Singer* was billed as the first feature-length talkie), was frenetic. Actors really hammed up the action by exaggerating each movement and contorting their faces to wring out every ounce of emotion. It made an art of artifice.

Chaplin, meanwhile, adopted a more organic approach – he would walk in and out, walk around the scene, and feel his way into the drama. A technique we are all familiar with now: improvisation.

Chaplin was born in the era of vaudeville and had spent his early years performing in variety shows alongside jugglers, magicians and singers. It was high-octane entertainment with one act after another and another. When he stepped into a more nuanced style of acting, and particularly directing, it heralded revolution through evolution.

It is possible to be inspirational without breaking the mould, and maybe valuing what you have and your heritage can actually be useful, crucial even, in creating something that is dazzlingly dynamic and progressive.

31
TAKE THE ROUGH WITH THE SMOOTH

'As a young lad breaking through you have to wait for your chance.'

HARRY KANE

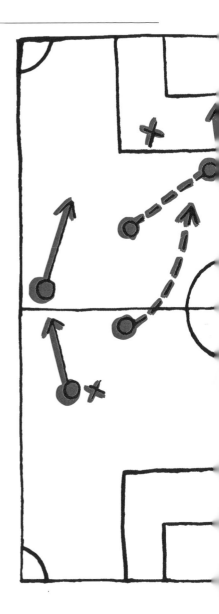

They say that football is a game of two halves – it may seem blindingly obvious but there is a deeper philosophy underpinning the cliché. That more profound meaning is that life, as in football, can switch around completely. At one moment you're on a roll, everything is going well, you're invincible. Then, without warning, wham! You're lost. The game, your life, everything hovers on the brink of disaster.

In 2015, the Professional Footballers' Association crowned

Londoner Harry Kane as their Young Player of the Year, in recognition of his sensational scoring and his superb skills, uncommon for a player of only 21. No one could have predicted the Tottenham Hotspur striker's stellar rise to become one of the world's best players. Certainly not Arsenal Football Club, Tottenham's north London rivals. They had spotted his potential and taken the eight-year-old Kane into their junior squad. But within 18 months the Gunners, unimpressed, released him.

Thankfully, the damage to Kane's self-esteem was not permanent. It wasn't long before Spurs signed Kane to their youth squad, nurturing and developing him, to be rewarded by the fully fledged player who is now a goal-making machine. He was the top scorer in the 2015/16 Premier League with a goal tally of 25, and shoots for England at international level too.

It's a funny old game, football. Life, too. Both can be seen as a beautiful, glorious game. Fortunately, our lives have more than two 45-minute halves. So next time you are metaphorically sitting on the subs' bench, remember, your call-up to glory is only seconds away.

32
BELIEVE IN YOURSELF

'If the people in charge are very egotistical...
consciously or unconsciously they will
discourage creativity in other people.'

JOHN CLEESE

What is self-belief? It may be hard to define but we all know just how vital it is, and how damaging *not* having self-belief can be. Without it, we can be plagued by doubts, whether in our personal or professional lives. Am I good enough? How will people react if I do or say this? I don't want to be seen as a failure so I'd better just keep my head down. If you recognise any of these thought patterns then what you're doing, unwittingly, is handing over your power, your right to success and happiness. Yes, you are giving up your claim to a bright and fulfilling future.

When attempting to step 'outside of the norm', self-belief can often be the only asset you have in the beginning. It is your engine, your comfort in hard times. How much self-belief do you think you need to muster in order to break into one of the creative industries? Truckloads. And then some.

John Cleese – comic genius, the man of funny walks, absurd humour and Monty Python fame – nearly didn't become a household name when he submitted a sample script for a new sitcom called *Fawlty Towers* to the BBC. Script editor Ian Main wrote in a memo to his boss that the script was 'as dire as its title', full of 'clichés and stock characters'. He predicted it would be a 'disaster'. How wrong! The series became a cult classic, thanks to the then Head of BBC Comedy and Light Entertainment James Gilbert, who gave it the green light.

Cleese has continued to create comedy gold and has made millions of us laugh for over 40 years. So, if you believe in something, and believe in yourself, don't be put off by hurtful rejection.

In the words of Eleanor Roosevelt: *'No one can make you feel inferior without your consent.'*

At school you can get stuck with all sorts of labels – not all of them positive. Whether it's being called the 'class clown', 'a noisy nuisance' or 'a troublemaker', such labels can stick like glue; they can hamper your development and blight your future.

Or maybe not… Take one of the 20th century's most revered individuals – Sir Winston Churchill. Some claim he was Britain's greatest ever prime minister, and most would agree that he proved to be a titanic leader at a critical time in the country's history. Alas, his talents didn't shine through at school, St George's in Ascot, where his end-of-year report noted that he *'is a constant trouble to everybody and is always in some scrape or other. He cannot be trusted to behave himself anywhere.'*

Mercifully, Churchill was undaunted by such criticism. The saying 'cometh the hour, cometh the man' is the perfect way to describe Winston Churchill as he stepped into the political breach to lead the country during the difficult years of the Second World War, when European nations lined up in conflict against each other. His staunch defence against aggressors, his rousing speech-making – *'I have nothing to offer but blood, toil, tears and sweat'* – and dogged determination have assured him a very special place in history. And he led the Allies Forces to victory.

Churchill's political career lasted over 60 years; he inspired a nation and was a great wartime leader. There is much we can learn from his example: don't be pigeon-holed; don't allow yourself to be confined by someone else's idea of who you are, what you are and what you can do.

33
BREAK THE MOULD

'No boy or girl should ever be
disheartened by lack of success in their
youth but should diligently and faithfully
persevere and make up for lost time.'
WINSTON CHURCHILL

'I could have given up. I had depression, everything. But I felt in my heart one day it might happen...
'All the ups and downs I've had, I think they've made me the athlete I am. It made me stronger. I've had every single emotion an athlete can have.'
KELLY HOLMES

34 OVERCOME HURDLES

Coping strategies vary a lot from person to person. Some people hum as a way of alleviating stress (though, beware, this can be irritating for others in the workplace!). A less potentially disruptive method might be deep-breathing exercises.

Perhaps one of the most extreme coping mechanisms is when a person resorts to self-harming. This is not the preserve of only teenagers or young adults. There is a surprising number of people of all

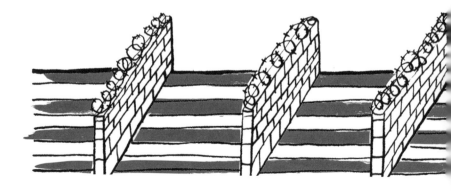

ages who self-injure. For some who need to release tension and combat demons, this is the only way.

Olympic champion Kelly Holmes is revered for her double gold medal win at the 2004 Athens Games. She had enjoyed successes over the years but her career as a middle-distance runner had been blighted by injury, and the medals eluded her as the fitness problems mounted.

Her achievements in Athens can be seen as the pinnacle of her career, thrilling the nation and sports fans around the globe. But the double gold medal winner was troubled, and a year before her Olympic triumph Kelly Holmes was self-harming. Her training schedule was punishing, her body suffered, and the nagging fear of failure, of not been quite good enough on the world stage, was lurking. *'Things get on top of you. Something chemically happens.'*

Fast-forward to 2016: Kelly Holmes completed the London Marathon in an impressive 3 hours 11 minutes, raising much-needed funds for grateful charities. She is a healthier Kelly in every way, more robust mentally and able to cope with setbacks and failures without thoughts of self-harming or suicide.

Kelly Holmes – who was made a Dame in 2005 – remains an inspiration to us all, not just on the track, but in life generally. She illustrates that demons can be tamed, that we can abolish self-loathing and self-punishment from our repertoire, so that we too can continue to participate in the marathon of life.

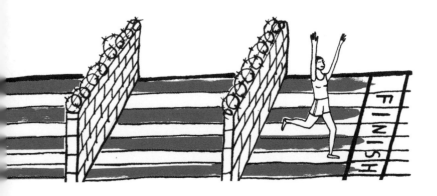

35

'EACH OF YOU HAS
A DISTINCTIVE VOICE...
WHEN YOU FIND IT,
YOUR STORY WILL BE TOLD.

YOU WILL

BE HEARD.'

JOHN GRISHAM

36
KNOW WHEN TO QUIT

'Even when you are successful and riding high and top of your game, you can fail.'
CHRIS EVANS

How do you redeem yourself in the eyes of loved ones, family, friends and millions of total strangers who know you only through the medium of radio and TV?

To be in the public eye means to be scrutinised mercilessly. Any slip-ups, or falls from grace, seem to be seized upon and enjoyed far more than the success stories.

Chris Evans is the paperboy from Warrington, in Lancashire, who became a multi-millionaire. As a teenager he saw his father pass away and he recalls how that became a big driver for 'making it'.

One success is not an automatic passport to another. You have to admire DJ Chris Evans for being brave, not resting on his laurels or being complacent as host of the UK's favourite and most successful radio breakfast show. He accepted what some might think was a poisoned chalice – the opportunity to take over Jeremy Clarkson's *Top Gear* throne.

When Chris Evans took on the challenge to become Clarkson's successor on the wildly popular TV show, it seemed like a match made in heaven. With Chris's obsession with everything cars, what could possibly go wrong? It all sounded good on paper but sometimes, for some reason, the suit just doesn't fit. He didn't gel with the *Top Gear* audience and the critics slaughtered him after the first programme, saying he was the wrong guy for the job.

There was a time when the young, rebellious Evans might have reacted differently. He might have thought he was invincible and just disappeared on a 17-hour pub crawl to drown his disappointment. But with age comes wisdom and, no matter how brilliant and creatively talented you are, sometimes you just have to accept that, despite your best efforts, you crashed. Exiting with grace and honesty, as Chris did, does at least leave your dignity intact.

We admire youth for its energy, optimism and adventurousness. We tend to think of daring, innovation and fresh thinking as being the preserve of the young. We are statistically more likely to 'stay put' when we mature. So risk-taking becomes a rarer feature the older we get.

The reason may be partly chemical: levels of the neuro-transmitter dopamine fall as we age. It has a role in moderating our reward-driven behaviour. Put simply, more dopamine means greater risk-taking to win the big prize; less dopamine means fewer risks are taken.

So it is something rather special when you become a huge success at the age of 40, in a field as fickle and faddish as the music business. But it happened to jazz singer Gregory Porter, he of the rich and captivating voice brimming with feeling.

He'd hoped to be an American pro football player and was on a sports scholarship when injury forced him out.

His singing had been confined to church and he was resigned to working in town planning, a respectable job for Porter who was one of nine children raised single-handedly by their heroic mother. But even the church singing stopped after his mother died from breast cancer.

The sadness was eventually broken. Porter, recalling his mother's words on her death bed, *'Don't forget music, it's the best thing you do'*, returned to singing. In what seemed like no time at all, he had won the highest music award – a Grammy – for the album *Liquid Spirit.*

So if life feels like it's passing you by, if you feel you've let your one big chance slip and you too must resign yourself to a safe work role, think again. Think about Gregory Porter's late entry into music, the huge acclaim he's received because he sings from the heart, and remember that authenticity comes from experience. His lyrics reflect every twist and turn in a complicated, far-from-easy existence, which can only be experienced; it cannot be learnt in an abstract way.

37
IT'S NEVER TOO LATE TO FIND ANOTHER DREAM

'You must experience
life before you sing it.'
GREGORY PORTER

38 CHOOSE YOUR LADDER

'I'm still pinching myself all the time at how the last few years have gone.'
JAMIE VARDY

When you are at the bottom of your career ladder, looking wistfully at the next rung and beyond, it would be reasonable to feel a little discouraged. Trying to get a toehold on the next step up can be a tiring

and protracted experience.

The idea of promotion becomes all-consuming, as we cogitate on the tactics and personal traits that we believe advancement requires. And it is of no comfort at all to hear, 'It's not about the destination; it's the journey that's important.'

Consider the journey of English Premier League footballer Jamie Vardy. He has gone from zero to

hero. Given the boot at sixteen by Sheffield Wednesday Football Club for being too small, he spent years pulling long shifts in a factory. He wore a tag for six months after defending his mate in a punch-up for which he was convicted of criminal assault. He maintained his love of football and was happy to play for the Stocksbridge Park Steels team on £30 a week.

Seven years on, in 2010, FC Halifax Town of the Northern Premier League came calling; they signed him for a fee of £15,000. A year later, Conference side Fleetwood Town snapped him up for a reported £150,000; and finally, in 2012, Leicester City in the Championship League paid £1 million for Vardy. Four years later, Vardy and the Foxes were crowned Premier League champions – it's been one heck of a ladder.

So, while we may balk at the idea of spending time at the bottom, sometimes that's where you get the perfect chance to observe, to learn through that observation and hone your craft. The pressure may be on, but perhaps not as much as on the big honcho teetering on the top rung. It's OK to be at the bottom of the ladder sometimes, as long as it's the right one for you.

39
BEAT THE
ODDS

'I don't want to sound arrogant, but I really think everything is achievable in life.'

NOVAC DJOKOVIC

Think your life is tough? Bemoaning your fate, and how life doesn't seem to be dealing you the best hand?

We know Novak Djokovic as a tennis champion, a man at the pinnacle of his career, hailed as one of the sport's all-time 'greats' – a tennis prodigy who is dominating the men's game. Born in Serbia, he was just six years old when his talent was spotted by Jelena Gencic, herself a sporting legend.

Hours of practice on lush courts to the sound of sweet birdsong? Not likely. This was the former Yugoslavia – Serbia's capital, Belgrade, where Djokovic was born, was in the throes of a brutal conflict.

The young Djokovic and his family would seek shelter in the

basement when the terrifying bombing raids were in full flow. His coach Gencic recalled choosing areas for practice that had been blitzed previously, her reasoning being that they were probably safe from another bombing, at least for a while.

He was a determined and committed novice who went on to become a world-beater. Even bombs couldn't prevent the boy from Belgrade from becoming a tennis titan.

Think about your own situation: is it really inhibiting your progress, sabotaging your success? Can anything be so bad that it stops you from becoming resilient and getting out there, as Djokovic did, to make your dream come true?

40 UGLY DUCKLINGS CAN BECOME SWANS

'I was a weird looking character... I never liked the way I would photograph.'

FRED ASTAIRE

We live in a time when talent increasingly takes a back seat to appearance. Across almost every genre, but especially in the creative industries, the pressure to look gorgeous is huge. It's not just women either. Men are feeling the heat of the hairdryer, the pain of waxing, the fascination of the facial. Indeed, young men today spend more on their grooming than women in the same age group.

But not all of the biggest successes in show business are easy on the eye. Look at Fred Astaire's dominance in the singing and dancing arena. He was not conventionally handsome, was rather slight, and his voice was thought to be on the thin side, but he danced like an angel, a craft honed over many years in vaudeville, touring with his sister Adele. Eventually he was called for a screen test with one of the major movie studios, RKO. The feedback was said to be damning, along the lines of: *'Can't act. Can't sing. Balding. Can dance a little.'*

David O. Selznick, the film executive who'd called Astaire in for the screen test, was disappointed but spotted something many hadn't. He wrote in a memo that *'in spite of his enormous ears and bad chin line… his charm is so tremendous'*.

Supreme talent and charisma can be just as potent generators of success as conventional good looks. Maybe it's a cliché, but many ugly ducklings do indeed become beautiful swans!

41
WHEN YOUR FACE DOESN'T FIT, CREATE A FIT FOR YOUR FACE

'I'm not everyone's cup of tea. But sometimes criticism can be hurtful. Be respectful; I'm a good piano player, I can sing well, I write good songs.'

ELTON JOHN

When it comes to securing a fantastic job, lucrative career or financial success – unless you're lucky enough to be a trustafarian – then seeking employment is the path you'll most likely take. It's a precarious one and not guaranteed to result in being hired. Defeat and rejection are commonplace.

Small comfort, then, to discover that, in terms of being recruited, your ability to do the job is only about 50 per cent of what's going on. The remainder is about personality, how well you come across in the interview and whether you would fit into the team or company. But don't take it personally – really, don't take it personally! You tried your best.

Consider superstar Elton John. He is a pop legend, a multi-award-winning performer and fabulously rich. But before his career really rocketed (once he teamed up with Bernie Taupin to become the phenomenal writing combo that created countless hits), Elton was still looking for a way into the music business. He attended numerous auditions for bands hoping that he'd get a break. One such try-out was with the group King Crimson, who are regarded as pioneers of the prog rock movement. In the end, it was decided that his singing style didn't fit the King Crimson sound, so they declined the services of the then unknown Elton. But what if that hadn't been the case? We could have had a very different-sounding star...

It's hard not to feel hurt when your face doesn't fit; a thumbs-down might seem like a direct insult but being rejected doesn't mean you're no good. Take the positives and be pleased that you got as far as you did. Consider too that if you – or in the case of Elton John, his voice – don't fit in, it could be a lucky escape. It wasn't meant to be. You might have had a terrible time there and not enjoyed the experience at all. Just remember – if your face doesn't fit, you're in good company!

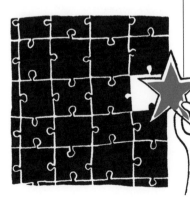

42

'HE WHO IS NOT COURAGEOUS ENOUGH TO

TAKE

RISKS

WILL ACCOMPLISH NOTHING IN LIFE.'

MUHAMMAD ALI

We don't arrive on this earth exactly the same as everyone else. Our learning and development rates are so different and comparisons with others are often invidious.

A late bloomer is a person with talents or skills that may not be apparent to others until later than usual. The name 'Einstein' is synonymous with genius on a scale that is rare, but his early years were spent behind the pack rather than leading it. He was a slow starter and is thought not to have uttered a word until he was four. School life was not for him either and he left without completing his education.

But that didn't stop him from his pursuit of science or from being dubbed the 'father of modern physics'. In fact, Einstein single-handedly revolutionised the field of physics and gave us one of the most beautiful equations in the world, $E = mc^2$, to boot. He remains iconic and even topped a *Time* magazine 'Person of the Century' poll in 1999.

Take heart if you are not on track with your peers. Self-development and maturity take time; they can't be scheduled. Stop and think about whether following a timeline really suits you, or does it make you uncomfortable? Knowledge comes in many forms.

43
BE A LATE DEVELOPER

'Imagination is more important than knowledge. For knowledge is limited… while imagination embraces the world.'
ALBERT EINSTEIN

44 NEVER GIVE UP

We all have the need to be endorsed and feel supported. Approval from our family or wider community means that what we are doing is right and good, doesn't it? And it adds to our feeling of security and wellbeing.

So if this approval is withheld, we can suddenly feel vulnerable, stressed, even unhappy. It may force us to change direction, or drop an idea or belief in an effort to win back the affection of those around us.

Movie director George Lucas sought support from the film community for a project that some thought was simply too outlandish. Had he bowed to their disapproval, one of cinema's greatest movie franchises would never have existed.

In 1977, *Star Wars* changed the movie world, revived the sci-fi genre

'If you want to be successful in a particular field, perseverance is one of the key qualities.'

GEORGE LUCAS

and set a new benchmark for special effects. But director George Lucas, fresh from the success of *American Graffiti*, didn't have an easy time convincing the major studios to back him and the project. Science fiction was considered a dodo, a dead genre and a bit of a joke.

He took the idea round the major studios, who all turned it down. But he never gave up. Finally, Alan Ladd Jr at 20th Century Fox took

a punt on the project. It was a leap of faith which has been amply rewarded. Not a flop, but a billion-dollar franchise was born.

If you are passionate about an idea that you wish to bring to fruition, keep the faith and endeavour to find the right support – it may be the start of something magnificent and magical. May the force be with you!

45
DRAW STRENGTH FROM PAIN

'My dad never did hugging, never said, "I love you".'
LENNY HENRY

What is the most powerful force on earth? Is it atomic energy, the awesome oceans? Or is it that simple four-letter word – love?

When we're growing up, our reliance on the adults around us is huge. We are vulnerable and need nurturing. As well as being watered and fed, we need to be emotionally nourished too. A paucity of affection can not only upset us, it can also do us serious damage. Did you have enough love?

It's a curious situation that one of the UK's most-liked and respected comics is a man who felt under-loved. Lenny Henry has opened up about the extent of his emotional neglect. *'It wasn't until my mum was poorly near the end of her life that we started saying, "I love you, I love you, I love you."'*

One of seven children born to

Jamaican immigrant parents, life was tough, with both his dad and mum working hard, physically hard, as a factory worker and seamstress respectively. Deprived of affection when growing up, Lenny Henry has carried the emotional scars with him. He's mourned the love he never felt and yet been able to reflect on the circumstances of his home life. He learnt too that the man he called 'Dad' wasn't his biological father.

According to Lenny, *'My upbringing gave me a lot of backbone and prepared me well for showbiz. It could throw anything at me and I could take it.'*

It is so important to work to understand the pain of childhood especially, and not let it stunt development. Recognising the hurt allows for grieving to take place, and sets you on the path to actually taking control of it.

She is the billionaire queen of American daytime TV. Oprah Winfrey is adored by millions and regarded as being ethical, brave, generous and talented.

Her success extends beyond being a TV personality; she is an award-winning actress, too. But the comfort and fame enjoyed in later life are in sharp contrast to her humble origins. She grew up dirt poor, she was abused as a child and suffered the unspeakable heartbreak of giving birth when just 14 to a son who died in infancy.

She has shrugged off her poverty and the hardships of her early life to evolve her own philosophy and become a household name.

As Oprah has said: *'It's not where you come from that matters – it's where you want to go.'*

Imagine yourself in a new role, looking happy and being capable. We may not all end up as celebrated and fabulously wealthy as Oprah, but she should remain a shining example of what we can all achieve if we refuse to be a victim, paralysed by a sense of unworthiness or shame. Thank you, Oprah.

46
REFUSE TO BE A VICTIM

'Turn your wounds into wisdom.'
OPRAH WINFREY

47
KEEP
GOING

'Having had cancer, one important thing to know is you're still the same person at the end.'

KYLIE MINOGUE

The petite, loveable Australian pop princess, Kylie Minogue, has entertained us through the decades with consistent hits. Her songs have touched the public's consciousness – from the 1988 UK debut smash 'I Should Be So Lucky' to the hypnotic 2001 number one single 'Can't Get You Out of My Head'.

Kylie Minogue is the consummate professional and is known for her spectacular concerts. It was during her sold-out Showgirl world tour in 2005 that she faced the biggest battle of her life when diagnosed with breast cancer, which forced her to cancel the Australian leg. She likened her cancer battle and chemotherapy to experiencing a nuclear bomb and said that she was

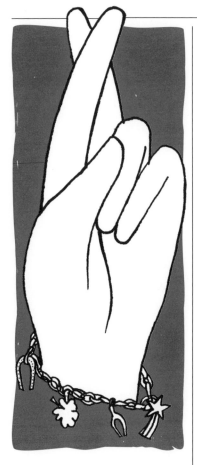

determined to resume her career.

Kylie was as good as her word and 18 months later she was back on stage in Sydney with the Showgirl: The Homecoming Tour, joking with the audience that she was 'fashionably late'. It was a highly emotional concert for her and she cried before dedicating the song 'Especially for You' to her father, a survivor of prostate cancer.

Illness takes no account of how successful you are; it doesn't discriminate between famous and ordinary, rich and poor. So when you are in a position of power and influence, like Kylie, openly sharing your experiences, both good and bad, with others in a similar predicament offers hope and inspiration.

48
OVERCOME YOUR
OBSTACLES

'I was a smart kid, and had a lot to say, but I just couldn't say it. It would just haunt me. I never thought I'd be able to sit and talk to someone...'

EMILY BLUNT

She's known for her great diction and clipped British accent acquired from attending public schools. She's played a young Queen Victoria, a snooty fashion assistant opposite Meryl Streep in *The Devil Wears Prada*, and taken the lead role in *The Girl On The Train*. Emily Blunt is a phenomenal actress at ease on screen and with any script, but her early years were very different.

Emily had a disabling stammer inherited from her barrister father's side of the family. Conversations were difficult and trying, and punctuated by her stammering. Speech therapy sessions and relaxation techniques saw little improvement in her chronic condition.

Her mother had had a career in acting before marrying and starting

a family, but for young Emily, thoughts of a future career reliant on being a dazzling speaker never entered her head.

A teacher eventually encouraged Emily into acting with a very handy, life-changing tip, which was to adopt an accent on stage. It had a radical effect.

'I distanced myself from me through this character, and it was so freeing that my stuttering stopped when I was onstage. It was really a miracle.'

Childhood conditions impact hugely on our young, developing selves. The cause is not always clear, making the experience unsettling and even frightening. How incredible and encouraging to know that a tongue-tied, hesitant and faltering young girl is now a famous, successful Hollywood A-list actress!

49

'I HAVE THE SAME

GOAL I'VE HAD EVER

SINCE I WAS

I WANT

A GIRL: TO RULE THE WORLD.'

MADONNA

In retrospect, we would all do some things differently, and this is certainly the case with Jack Ma. The self-made billionaire is not your typical success story.

Raised in poor, communist China, Ma's tale is one of rags to riches. He trained in China and initially became an English high school teacher, then without any business background went on to become an e-commerce billionaire.

The definition of a true trier, Ma was undaunted by rejection and failure. Turned down by prestigious Harvard university 10 times, failing three college entrance exams and rejected from 30 jobs – including fast food chain KFC! – he refused to be disheartened.

He started his business from his home by raising over $60,000 with a group of 18 friends to create Alibaba. The billion dollar online ecommerce website group has more than 400 million active buyers in over 190 countries.

Ma may be slightly disingenuous when he says, *'My biggest mistake was that I made Alibaba. I never thought*

that this thing would change my life.' He laments how busy he is running this vast and ridiculously booming enterprise. *'Every day is like as busy as a president, and I don't have any power! And then I don't have my life.'*

But there is a sombre message running through his railing against his success, which is that if he could start again he would give business a wide berth. *'In my next life, if I still can have a next life, I will never do a business like this. I will be my own self. I want to enjoy my life.'*

We hear a lot about the work/life balance and how crucial it is to strike the right mix of work and play in order to be happy and healthy. It isn't easy to find a healthy equilibrium between the two, and no one, not even billionaires, is immune from the deep discontent that comes from an inequality between the two. Reassess what you think success means. Are you happy, healthy and loved? Then perhaps striving for more money, a bigger house and more possessions isn't so important.

50
REDEFINE SUCCESS

'No matter how successful you are in your
career, you must always remember that
we are here to live. If you keep yourself
busy working, you will surely regret it.'

JACK MA

51
LET CRITICISM BE YOUR TEACHER

'Some actors couldn't figure out how to withstand the constant rejection. They couldn't see the light at the end of the tunnel.'
HARRISON FORD

How do you feel when you're being criticised? Embarrassed, angry, deflated? Negative feedback can be destructive, and it can feel maliciously personal. Or do you see it as a positive sign of interest that someone is bothering to tell you what they think?

Criticism can present a golden opportunity to learn, either about yourself or the person doing the critiquing. What do they want from you? If it's your boss, then it really is

worth knowing.

Way before Harrison Ford became a huge movie star through his roles as Han Solo in *Star Wars* and Indiana Jones in *Raiders of the Lost Ark*, he was just another Hollywood hopeful trying to break into acting. He was signed to a major studio, Columbia Pictures, on their 'New Talent' programme, working as an extra – often in non-speaking roles.

His actual film debut came in 1966 when he played the part of a

bellhop in *Dead Heat on a Merry-Go-Round*. It was a huge opportunity, a chance to shine, especially as his scene is with legendary actor James Coburn, and he got to speak some lines. It's a 30-second sequence, and yet it was enough for one movie exec to declare the young Harrison Ford a flop. Producer Jerry Tokofsky told Ford he just didn't have what it takes, saying that the first time Tony Curtis appeared in a film he was dropping off a bag of groceries –

but he did it like a movie star! Then came his critique of Ford's on-screen presence: *'You ain't got it, kid! Get back to class, because you ain't going to work in this studio for six months, maybe a year.'*

If, like Harrison Ford, you can take criticism on the chin, it may actually be helpful. Ford didn't crumble when faced with this seemingly withering assessment of his potential. He carried on to enjoy one of Hollywood's most enduring careers, spanning six decades – that's how to respond to criticism!

In our 'show and go' world, it is admirable to see longevity in any field, especially music.

In the late 70s, Chris Difford and Glenn Tilbrook of pop group Squeeze were lauded among the best songwriting duos, in the same breath as Lennon and McCartney, Elvis Costello and Elton John and Bernie Taupin. Heady stuff for the New Wave band.

The pair wrote all their own songs, which are boisterous and poignant, reflecting contemporary life from a very personal viewpoint. You see this in songs such as 'Take Me I'm Yours' and 'Up The Junction'. As Chris Difford has observed, *'I think songwriting is a therapy… the writing desk is like the psychiatrist's chair.'*

One of their biggest hits is 'Cool For Cats', but it was a struggle for Chris Difford to get the lyrics to fit the music. He described himself as being 'blocked' when it came to nailing the song. To ease the frustration, he made some cheese on toast and settled down to watch a bit of TV. On came comedian Benny Hill singing his comedy cum novelty song 'Ernie (The Fastest Milkman In The West)', which topped the charts in 1971. This was a eureka moment for Chris Difford, who took inspiration from the metre and elements of the song structure to complete 'Cool For Cats'.

We all need inspiration at times. It can be elusive, even fickle. One minute we're brimming with it and ideas are in full flow, then without warning it dries up. There's lots of advice out there about sources of inspiration, from TED talks to mood boards like Pinterest. But let's not overlook the everyday moments, like randomly tuning in to a television show and cracking the code to your bestselling song.

52 TAKE INSPIRATION FROM EVERYTHING

'It was really Benny Hill
that inspired "Cool For Cats".'
CHRIS DIFFORD

53 LEAN ON YOUR FAMILY

'If I could be half the dad that my dad was to me, that would be my best achievement.'

TOM DALEY

Still only in his early 20s, young and handsome, British Olympic diver Tom Daley is an inspiration to many. His aplomb on the diving board, and his openness about his sexuality has won him many fans around the globe.

As a twice-winning Olympic bronze medallist he epitomises dedication to his field, and is a true role model to all young would-be athletes.

Tom dedicated his winning performance at the 2012 London Olympic games to his dad, Rob, who sadly died from a brain tumour the year before, and so was denied his dream of seeing his son compete in the Olympics.

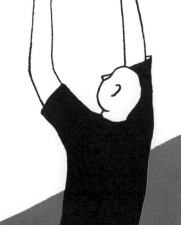

Tom said that every time he emerges from the water he expects to see his dad at the poolside, grinning and cracking jokes and making everyone around him laugh.

Belief and encouragement from your family is a winning component for success. The role your family can play in your success should not be underestimated. Family love can be especially powerful because at its purest and best, your well-being and happiness are their hope and priority. If you find that you are not spending enough time on your family relationships, you may want to rethink this. Family doesn't need to be blood relatives, but can be the friends who support you most in your life. Make time nurturing the tightest relationships in your life, no matter how busy you may feel at work: these are the people who are your support network.

54 HAVE DISCIPLINE

'You have to keep your bottom on the chair and stick it out, otherwise if you start getting to the habit of walking away when you're stuck, you'll never get it done.'

ROALD DAHL

A towering presence of a man at an imposing 6'5" (about 198 cm), Roald Dahl was a successful and beloved children's writer, one of the greatest storytellers of all time. His books are still bestsellers today from *Matilda* to *Charlie and The Chocolate Factory* and *The BFG* and *James and The Giant Peach*, to name just a few.

Roald Dahl wrote many of his books in a shed in his garden, sitting upon an old battered armchair. He balanced a specially designed writing board on his lap and wrote with an HB pencil on yellow legal pads. Dahl wrote daily, from 10 a.m. to 12 noon and then from 4 p.m. to 6 p.m. Every day, he would stick it out for two hours at a time with his bottom firmly stuck on his chair, only stopping after having reached his highest peak of concentration.

Discipline and regimentation without distraction works, and the retreat to a tiny hut at the end of his garden gave Dahl solace and time to concentrate, to let his ideas and imagination flow to produce timeless children's classics. If you are struggling to get an assignment done, get fit or find a new job, take a leaf out of Roald's book, and make it part of your routine. All successful people have habits and routines that have led to them achieving their goals. Write down a list of goals and take it from there.

55 DON'T USE AGE AS AN EXCUSE TO GET OLD

'If God is good enough to give you those years, flaunt them.'

IRIS APFEL

Iris Apfel describes herself as *'the world's oldest living teenager'* – and for good reason. The Manhattan style icon and former interior designer of the White House might be forgiven for taking a break now she's in her 90s, but Iris only seems to get busier and more vivacious.

Iris is feted for her unique sense of style. Always revered in fashion circles, she achieved widespread acclaim in 2006 at the age of 85, when the Metropolitan Museum of Art staged an exhibition showcasing her vibrant outfits and accessories.

She drew even more attention as the subject of Albert Maysle's 2014 documentary *Iris*, which allowed a new audience to admire her sharp wit and inspirational relationship with her beloved husband Carl. Sadly, Carl died in 2015, but Iris continues to take on new projects, including a line of wearable tech.

Remember, age is just a number. Don't use it as an excuse to be old before your time. The world can offer fresh excitement for everyone, whether you are a teenager or a pensioner. In Iris's wise words, *'The alternative to old is not very pleasant!'*

56
MAKE YOUR OWN RULES

'To me, business isn't about wearing
suits or pleasing stockholders. It's
about being true to yourself, your ideas
and focusing on the essentials.'

RICHARD BRANSON

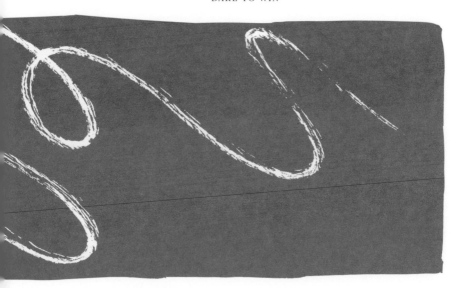

The Virgin brand touches our daily lives like no other: the Virgin name spans sectors from travel, transport, leisure, entertainment, telecoms and media, and comprises more than 400 companies.

It feels as if Virgin founder Richard Branson contemporised many aspects of our life by adding flourishes of style and comfort to travel, consumerism and leisure. He also taught us that we could do business differently and have fun along the way. His business acumen, charisma and downright likeability have wide appeal, and you can see his influence throughout his empire.

By throwing away the stiff suit and ditching the dull tie, he challenged workplace conventions and created an aura of excitement, creativity and inclusivity with his brands. Personally inspiring and motivating the workforce he forged a new paradigm in the commercial world, where customers felt allegiance to Virgin. They were excited to be involved in the enterprise through purchasing and consuming the tempting, cool products.

It takes character and strength to defy expectation. Do business in your own way and don't be restrained by convention.

57
LIVE WITHOUT LIMITS

'Tomorrow belongs to those
who can hear it coming.'
DAVID BOWIE

Ziggy Stardust could so nearly have played guitar and been 'jamming good' with Jemima and Humpty on children's TV show *Play School*.

There is truth in the expression that we get trapped in a job. Often, we find ourselves on a career path different to our real ambitions and try for jobs we really, in our heart of hearts, don't want to do. However, mortgages and bills have to be paid and the risk of losing security can mean unrealised dreams.

Many famous artists have auditioned for opportunities in their early days that fortunately did not pay off, fate having intervened and dealt a kind card. Before his success, David Bowie auditioned for the musical *Hair* as well as to be host of the BBC children's programme *Play School*.

'I don't see any boundaries between any of the art forms. I think they all inter-relate completely.'

Had he not been rejected, you do wonder what the impact of being a *Play School* presenter and sidekick to Little Ted might have been, and whether it would have damaged his credibility in the longer term.

The brilliance of David Bowie, his alter ego and continual self-reinvention, was destined to come through and his musical legacy will be eternally remembered.

Don't let yourself be trapped, even if you have to accept the distracting task of keeping a roof over your head... float for a while. Try to find ways of keeping focused, and other twisting-turning routes will eventually take you to your destination.